ESSENTIAL JAZZ ETUDES

BASS/TROMBONE

...The Blues

BASS/TROMBONE

by JACK WILKINS

Online Audio www.melbay.com/99576BCDEB

AUDIO CONTENTS

1	Tuning	14	Big Beat Blues
2	Blue Sax	15	Big Beat Blues - Rhythm Only
3	Blue Sax - Rhythm Only	16	Blue Caboose
4	Bridge Over Muddy Waters	17	Blue Caboose - Rhythm Only
5	Bridge Over Muddy Waters - Rhythm Only	18	BeBoppin' Alice
6	Big Blue Swing	19	BeBoppin' Alice - Rhythm Only
7	Big Blue Swing - Rhythm Only	20	Bouncing Blues
8	Slo' Mo' Blues	21	Bouncing Blues - Rhythm Only
9	Slo' Mo' Blues - Rhythm Only	22	Ursa Minor Blues
10	Too Sharp Blues	23	Ursa Minor Blues - Rhythm Only
11	Too Sharp Blues - Rhythm Only	24	Blues News
12	Bossa Blues	25	Blues News - Rhythm Only
13	Bossa Blues - Rhythm Only		

MEL BAY ®

I0809050

1 2 3 4 5 6 7 8 9 0

Table of Contents

Introduction

Welcome to *Essential Jazz Etudes*, by Jack Wilkins. This book with audio is designed for you to have a great time while improving your musical skills. Each etude teaches important musical lessons which you can apply to many other musical experiences. The audio recording features outstanding professional jazz musicians for you to listen to, learn from, and play along with! So get out your instrument, turn the audio on, and enjoy playing the etudes!

Tips for Getting the Most Out of Your *Essential Jazz Etudes* Book

Use the audio to help you learn the etude

1. Listen to the example track a few times.
2. Pick a short section to work on (12 bars or so).
3. Learn the notes, get the lines under your fingers.
4. Listen to the example track again for stylistic elements such as phrasing, articulation, dynamics, and sound.
5. Imitate the stylistic elements of the performer as well as you can.
6. Play the short section you are working on along with the example track.
7. When you feel pretty good about that section, take another short section and repeat steps 3-6.
8. Continue in this manner until you can play the entire etude along with the example track. Remember to try and imitate the stylistic elements as closely as possible.
9. Try playing the etude with the rhythm section accompaniment track. Listen to yourself play and give yourself a pat on the back for the things you are doing well. At the same time, determine what areas you need to improve in order to sound more like the example track. Listen to the example again and then give the accompaniment track another shot!
10. Have Fun!! This book was written for you to enjoy. By playing these etudes and listening to the recorded tracks, you will get better each time you pick up your instrument.

Some Other Tips

1. Many musicians like to start learning written music from the end, working their way back to the beginning in short sections (12 bars). That way, you will be adding the new sections you are working on to the ones you have already learned.
2. Practice difficult technical passages slowly, with a metronome. Strive for evenness of technique, however slowly you have to play to achieve that. Then speed the metronome up a few clicks at a time until you can play it at the same tempo you play the easier passages.
3. Jazz music requires dynamic articulations. Try to "overplay" the articulations at first, making the accented notes really stand out. You will get the feel for how jazz articulation works and how to make the etudes come alive by accenting certain notes and deemphasizing others.
4. One of the most important elements of jazz music is time feel. Much of the "feel" is generated by articulation, but the player has to "lock" the lines in time with the rhythm section. Listen to the rhythm section while you are playing and try to feel the 8th notes lining up with the groove they are playing. Most young players tend to rush the beat, actually playing faster than needed, so a good rule to live by is "RELAX!"

5. Playing along with the example tracks is a good opportunity to listen for INTONATION. Many wind instrumentalists tend to play sharp in the upper registers of their instrument.

6. Record yourself playing with the rhythm section tracks and listen back to the recording. Try to determine if you are playing with good articulation, sound, intonation and time feel. It is easier to hear what you sound like when you are not playing along. Work on fixing any problems and record yourself again. Congratulations! You are getting better!

7. Improvise with the rhythm section, trying to play in the style of the groove, and use the etude as an example of rhythms, phrases and note choices. Memorize short phrases you like from the etude and try to incorporate them into your own improvisations.

Chord Changes and Melodic Ideas

The chord changes for each etude are written, both on top of the etudes and as a chord sheet, with the chord changes over empty measures.

The changes over the written lines are there so you can understand how typical melodic lines sound with certain chord types and/or progressions. A chord progression is a series of chords that commonly occur in music. The 12-bar Blues is a common chord progression, with many variations. A shorter progression you will find in many of these blues progressions is the ii-V-I progression. It is found in many of these etudes in measures 9, 10, and 11. You can memorize lines from the etudes for these measures and try to place those lines into your improvisation in the same measure with the accompaniment. Once you hear how these ii-V-I phrases sound with the chord progression, try to improvise similar lines that flow through the chord progression. Use the same idea to create bluesy melodies for the first 4-8 bars of the blues. Note how the etudes use repetition and space to create phrases. Use the etude as a model for your improvisation while you get comfortable with the tune.

A chord sheet is included at the end of each etude. This shows you the form of the tune (usually a 12-bar blues in these etudes), and the chord progression. Here are a few useful practice ideas, which can help you improvise with the rhythm section.

1. Arpeggiate the chords. Try to arpeggiate root, 3rd, 5th, 7th 9th and back down. This type of arpeggiation is more typical of jazz music than triad arpeggios (root, 3rd, 5th, octave). Practice slowly, at a tempo which you can arpeggiate each chord in time, one after the other, for the form of the tune. Use a metronome and increase tempo slowly, like you did to learn the etude.

2. Learn scales that go with each chord. Practice these the same way you did arpeggios. Play the scale for the number of beats the associated chord is sounded. If a chord lasts for 1 measure, only play the scale for one measure, even if you have not finished the entire scale. If you are playing 8th notes, you can only play 8 notes for each measure, change to the next scale as the chords change. Once you can do this ascending from the root, try playing the scales down from the root. If you need more challenges, start on the 3rd, 5th, 7th or 9th, go up or down, or even alternate! This type of practice really helps you get a feel for keys and is invaluable in developing improvisation technique.

3. Try to mix up arpeggios, scales and some of the melodic ideas you like from the etudes. Make a game out of being able to play various combinations in time with the rhythm tracks. For instance: play four bars of arpeggios, the next four bars of scales, and the next four bars play a memorized line from the etude. Try one bar each, alternating arpeggios with scales, up and down, starting on various chord tones (root, 3rds, 5ths, etc). These practice games are challenging and fun and will improve your improvisational abilities quickly.

Common Chords and Scales Used in these Etudes

Dominant 7 chords (7) are the most used chords in these etudes, a chord that is very important to the sound of the blues. The following arpeggios and scales should be practiced in all keys and then used to help you improvise in the various dominant seven key areas found in the following etudes.

Dominant 7 Scale (Mixolydian mode)

Dominant 7 Bebop Scale

Dominant 7 Arpeggio to the 9th

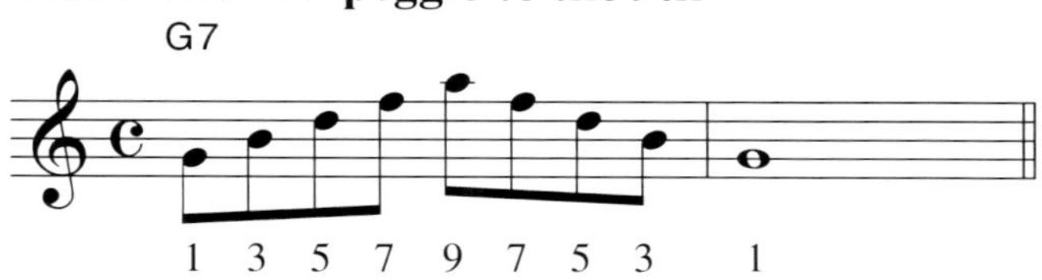

Dominant 7 Arpeggio Down from the 9th

Altered Dominant (7alt) – this is the type of dominant 7 chord found in minor keys, but is often used to color a V dominant chord in a major ii-V-I, or is used as a specific blues sound (during the melody of *Blue Caboose*, for example).

Altered Dominant Arpeggio/Line

Altered Dominant Scale (♭9, ♯9, ♯11, ♭13)

Minor 7 (m7) chords are found in these etudes as the ii chord of a ii-V-I, or in the minor blues tune *Ursa Minor Blues*.

Minor 7 Scale to the 9th (Dorian mode)

Arpeggio to the 9th

Arpeggio from the 9th

Major Seventh (Maj7) – this is the I chord in a major key, found in *Bebopppin' Alice* in this book.

Major 7 Arpeggio to the 9th

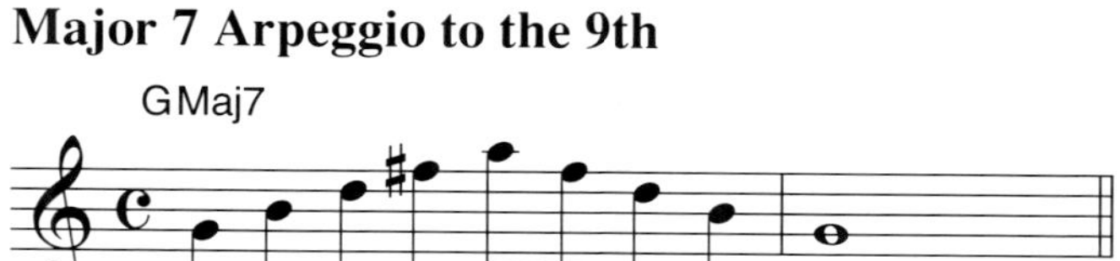

Major 7 Arpeggio from the 9th

Essential Blues and Pentatonic Scales

The Minor Pentatonic Scale and **Blues Scale** can be used to improvise melodic ideas for an ENTIRE 12-BAR BLUES. Unlike the scales and arpeggios listed above, which must change as the chords change, these "scales" provide a bluesy sound which fits over the entire chord progression. These scales are not really scales, but a group of notes used to create melodies. You don't have to use all of the notes of the scale to create good blues melodies. Listen as you improvise using these scales and try to hear which notes of the scale sound best with the different chords of the blues progression.

Repetition is a common device used to create blues melodies from the scales. Try to "sing" a melodic idea using these notes and then learn to play it. Many famous blues melodies utilize notes found in these scales. Of course it takes great skill, taste and experience (practice) to improvise really great blues lines using the minor pentatonic and blues scales. Start by creating your own blues melody, using repetition and space to create a 12-bar tune. Memorize it or write it down, and then create another new melody. Soon you will be able to create these types of melodies while improvising!

Minor Pentatonic and Blues Scales for Blues in G

G Minor Pentatonic "Scale"

G Blues "Scale" - pentatonic plus "blue" note (D♭) used to bend into note above (D) or below (C)

ii-V-I Progressions

The ii-V-I progression is a very important progression in jazz. Study the examples below and work on finding the ii-V-I areas in some of the etudes.

ii-V-I progression in the key of G major (arpeggios and scales based on G major scale)

ii-V-I progression in the key of G minor (arpeggios and scales based on G harmonic minor scale)

Blue Sax

2

3 Rhythm Only

Chord Progression

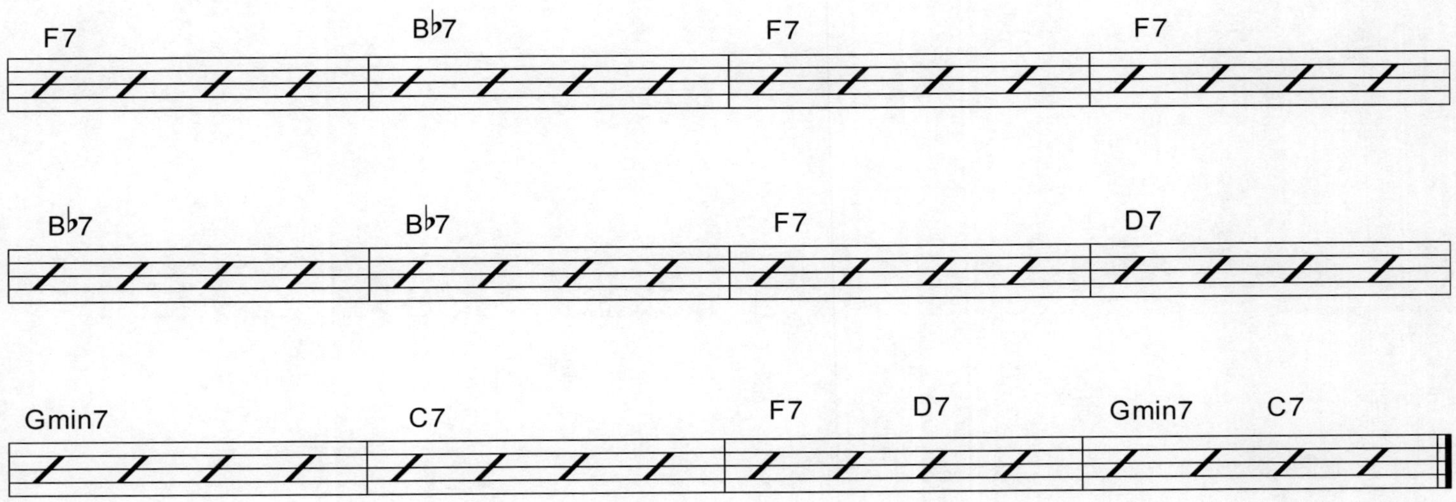

Bridge Over Muddy Waters

4

5 Rhythm Only

B♭7 E♭7 B♭7 B♭7
E♭7 E♭7 B♭7 B♭7 G7
Cmin7 F7 B♭7 G7 Cmin7 F7
B♭7 E♭7 B♭7 B♭7
E♭7 E♭7 B♭7 B♭7 G7
Cmin7 F7 B♭7 G7 Cmin7 F7
Bridge
A♭7 G7
F♯7 F7
B♭7 E♭7 B♭7
E♭7 E♭7 B♭7 B♭7 G7
Cmin7 F7 B♭7
TO TOP

Chord Progression

Bridge Over Muddy Waters

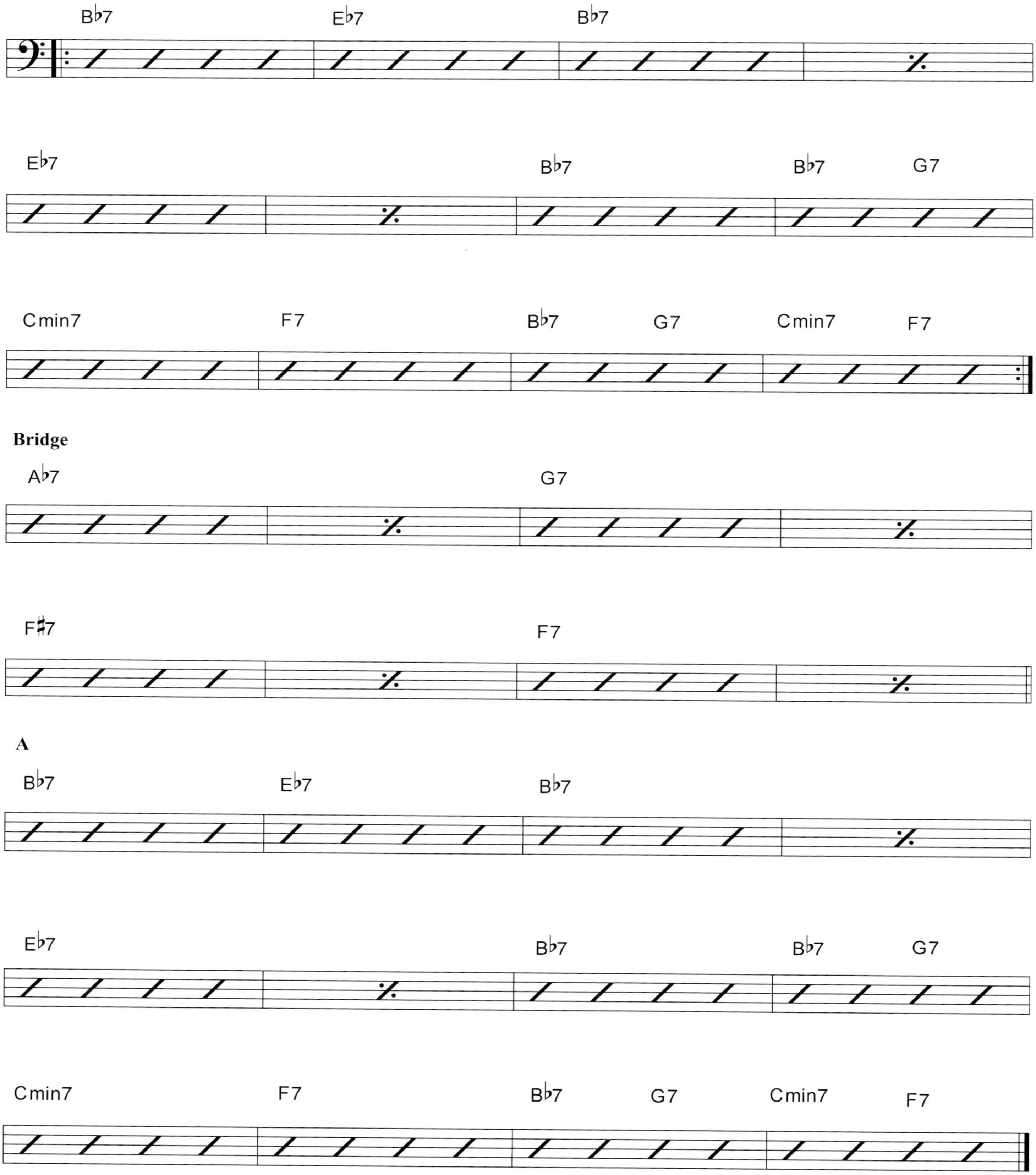

This page left blank intentionally to avoid awkward page turns

Big Blue Swing

disc 6

disc 7 Rhythm Only

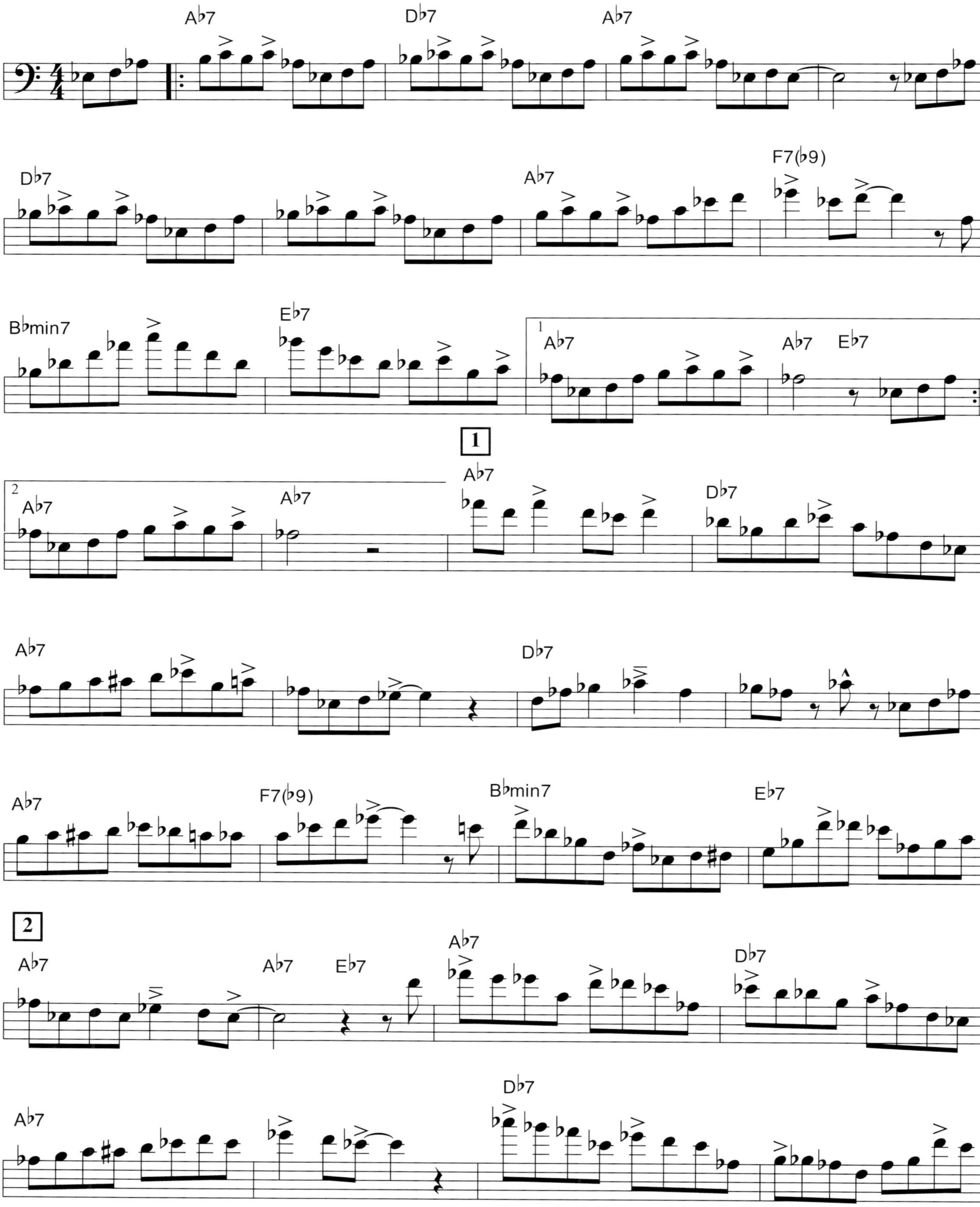

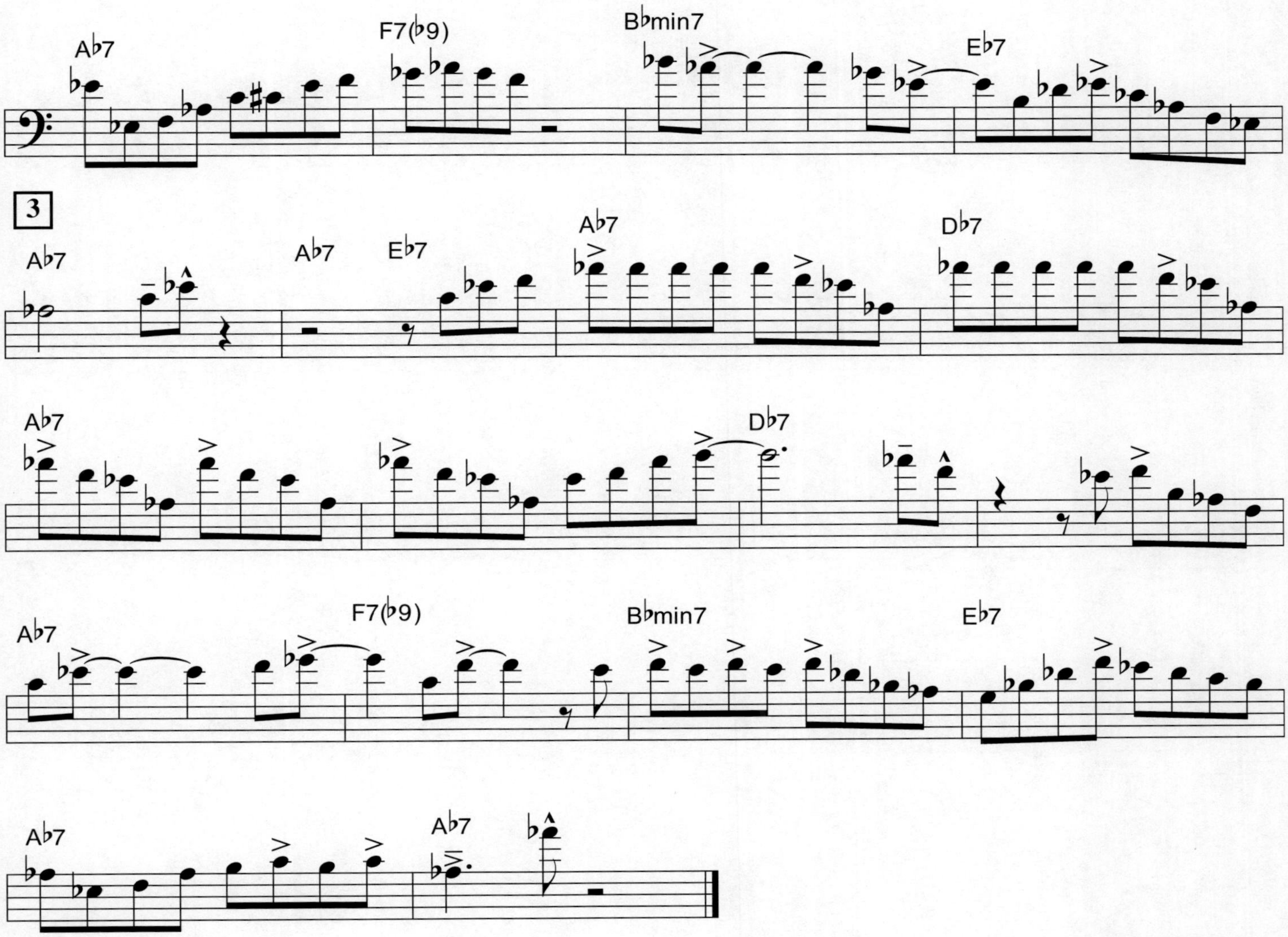

Chord Progression

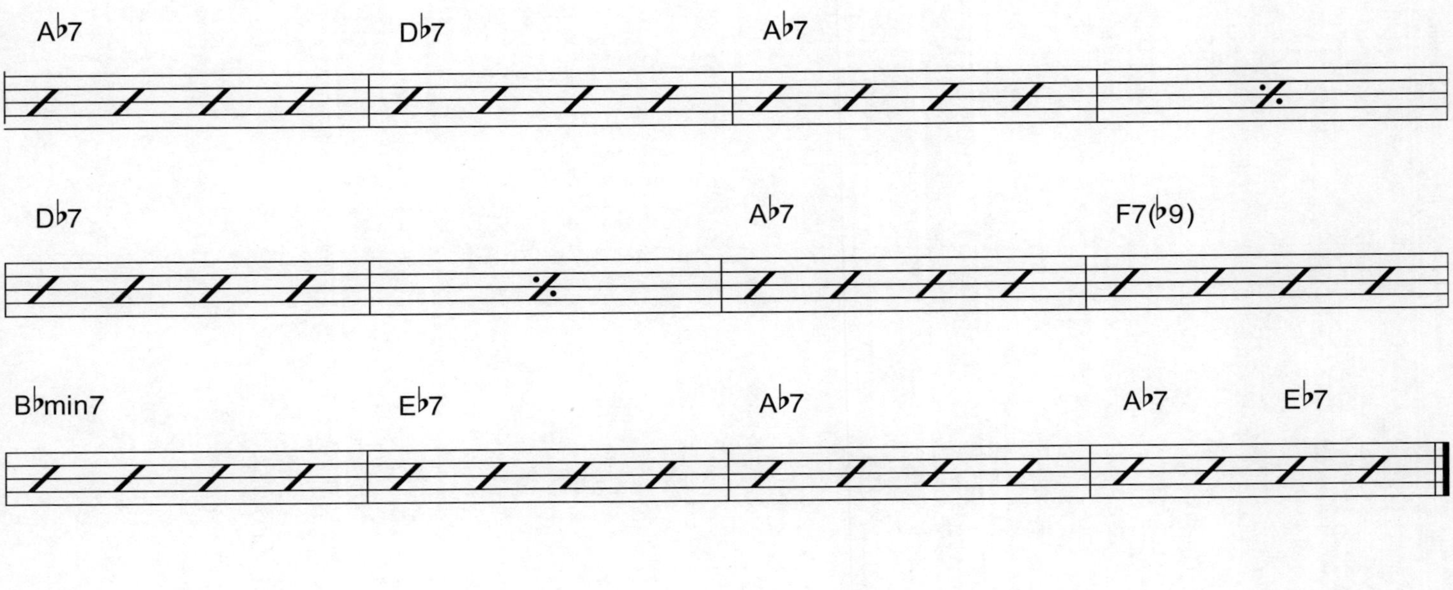

Slow Mo' Blues

8
9 Rhythm Only

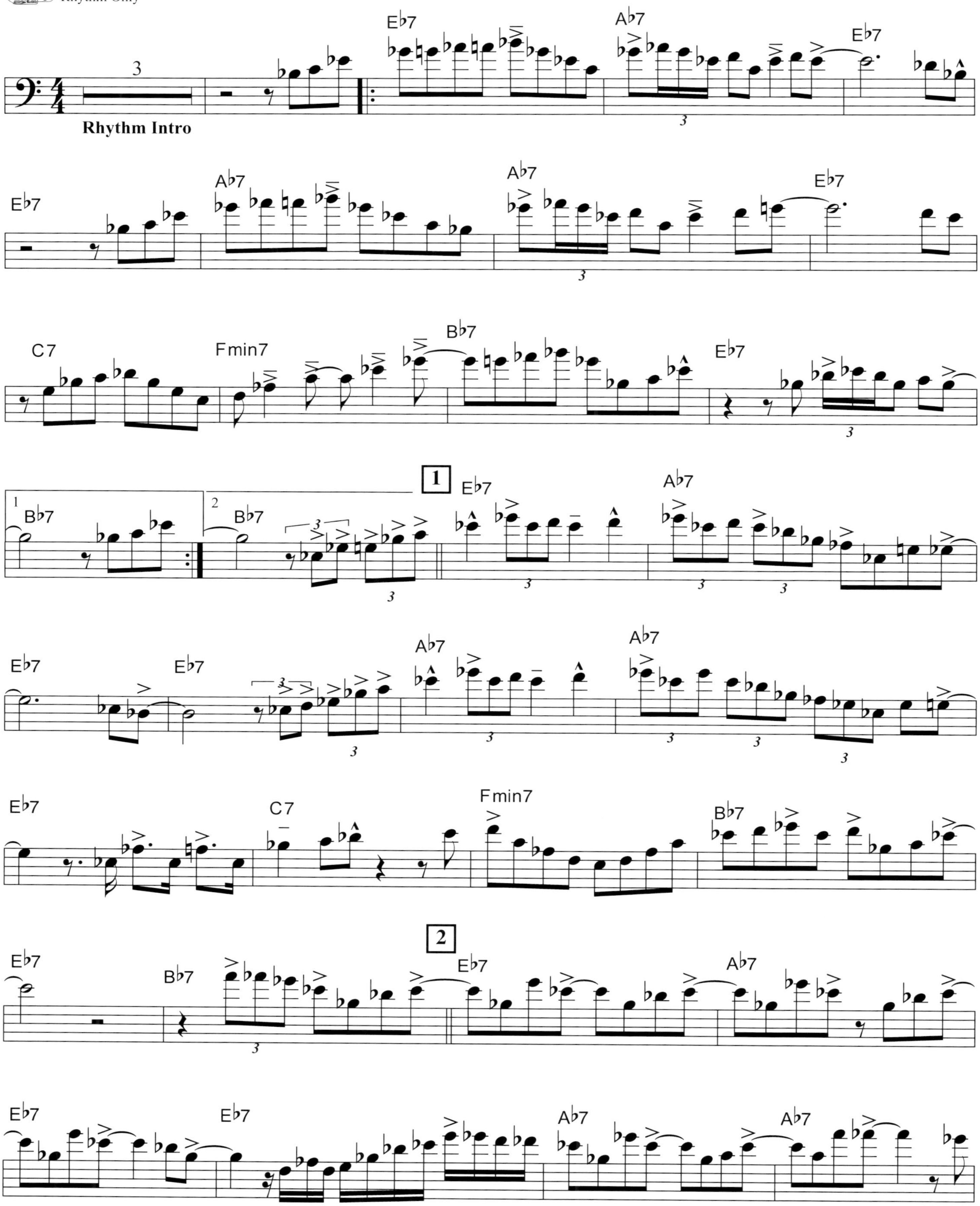

Chord Progression

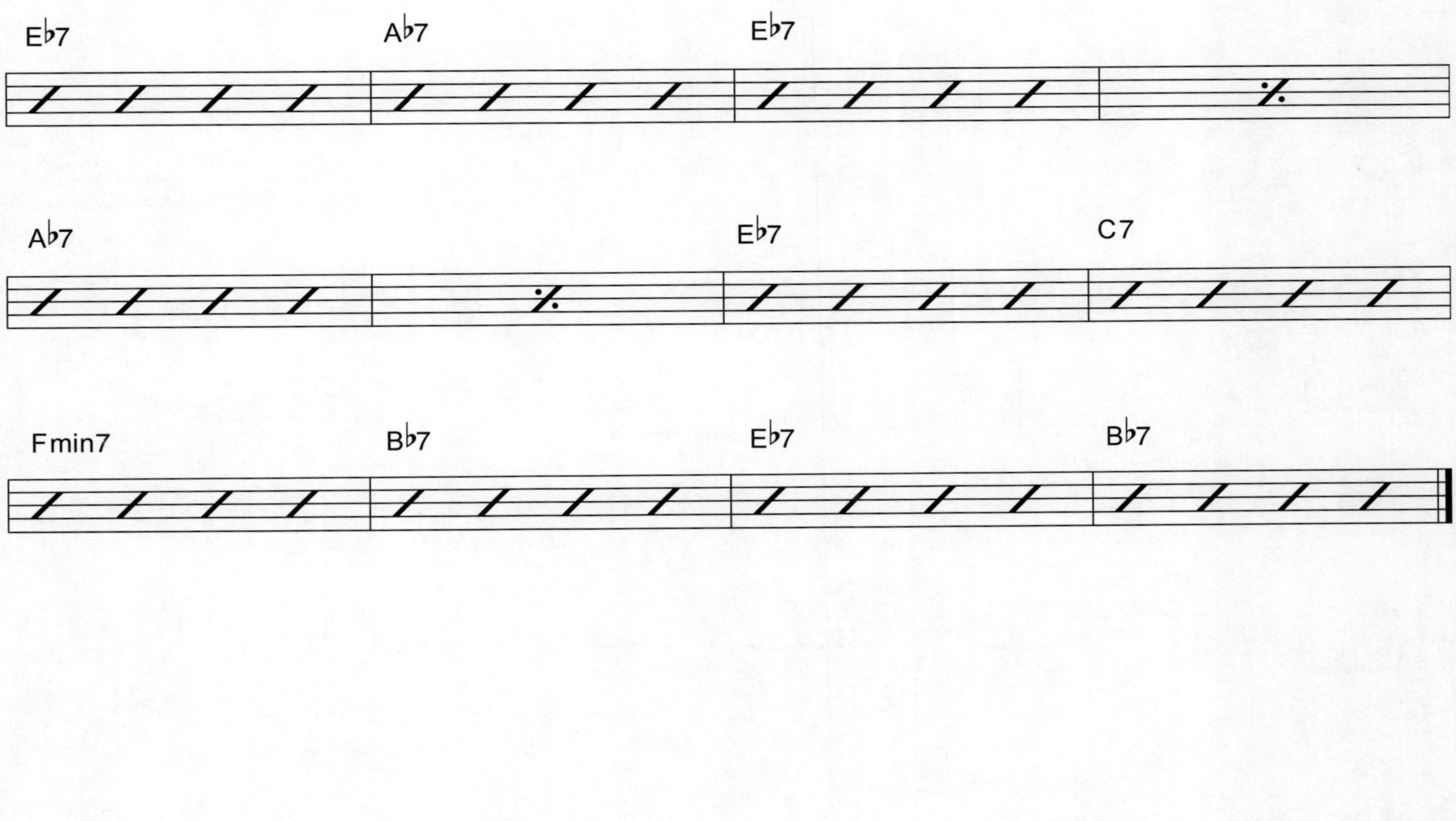

Too Sharp Blues

10
11 Rhythm Only

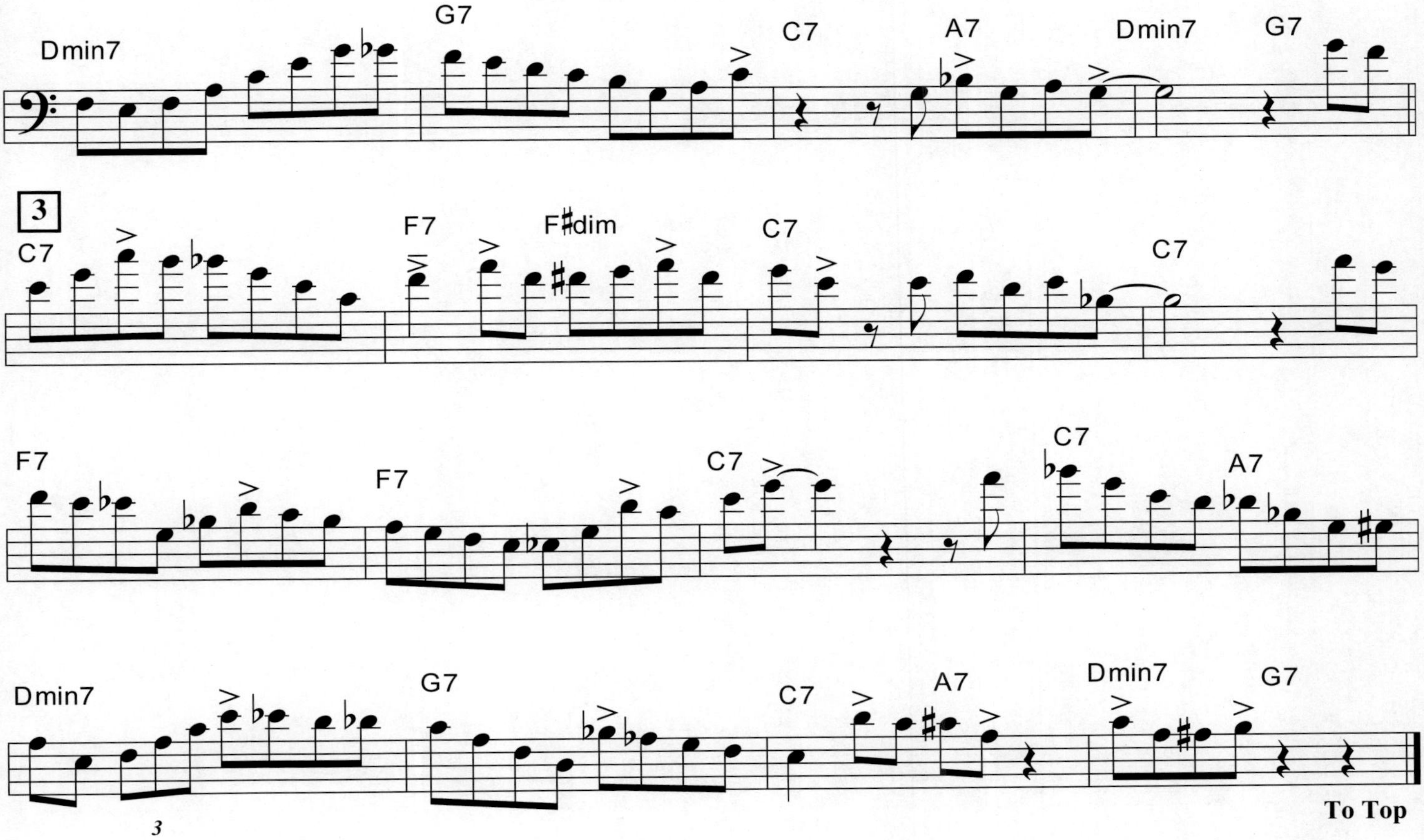

Chord Progression

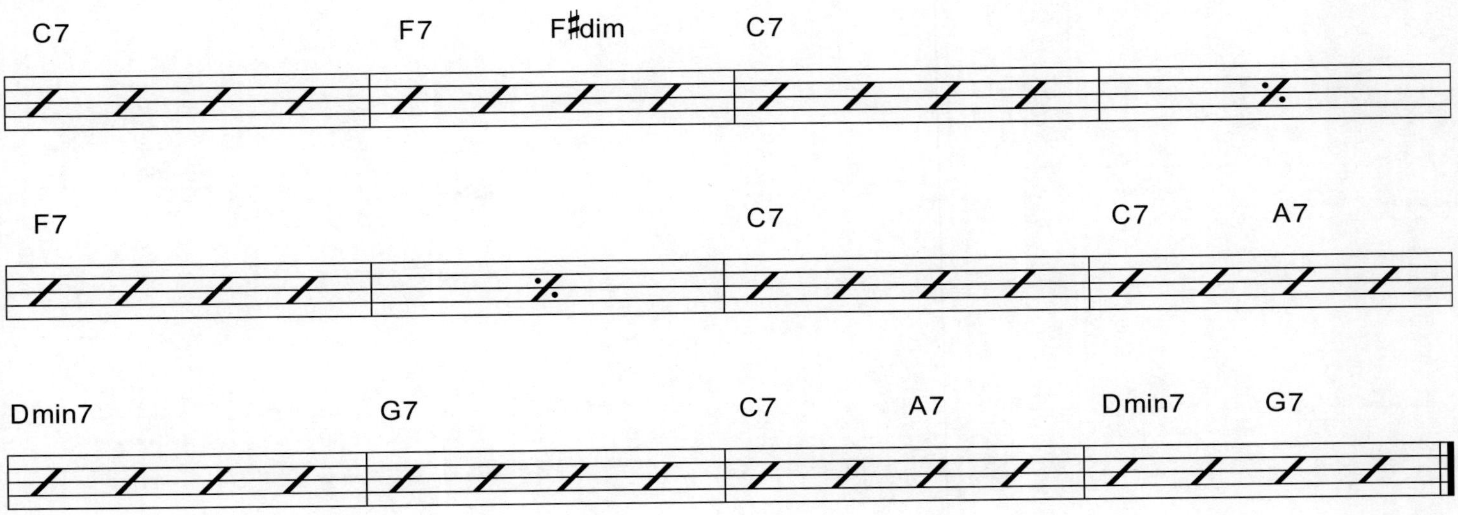

12
13 Rhythm Only

Bossa Blues

Chord Progression

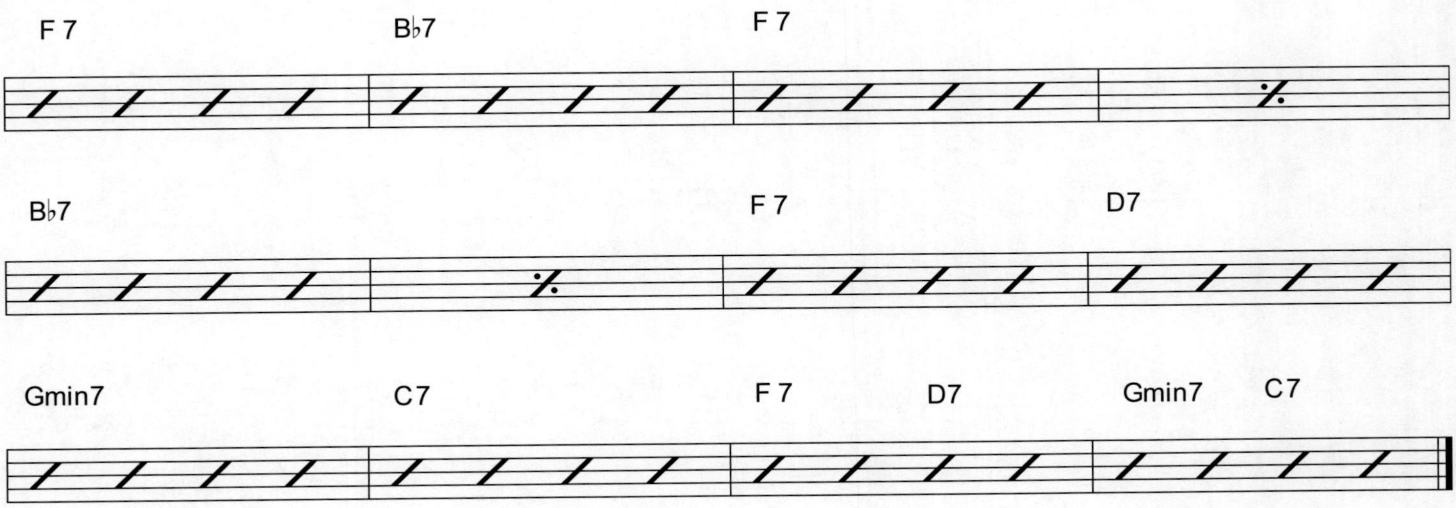

Big Beat Blues

14
15 Rhythm Only

Chord Progression

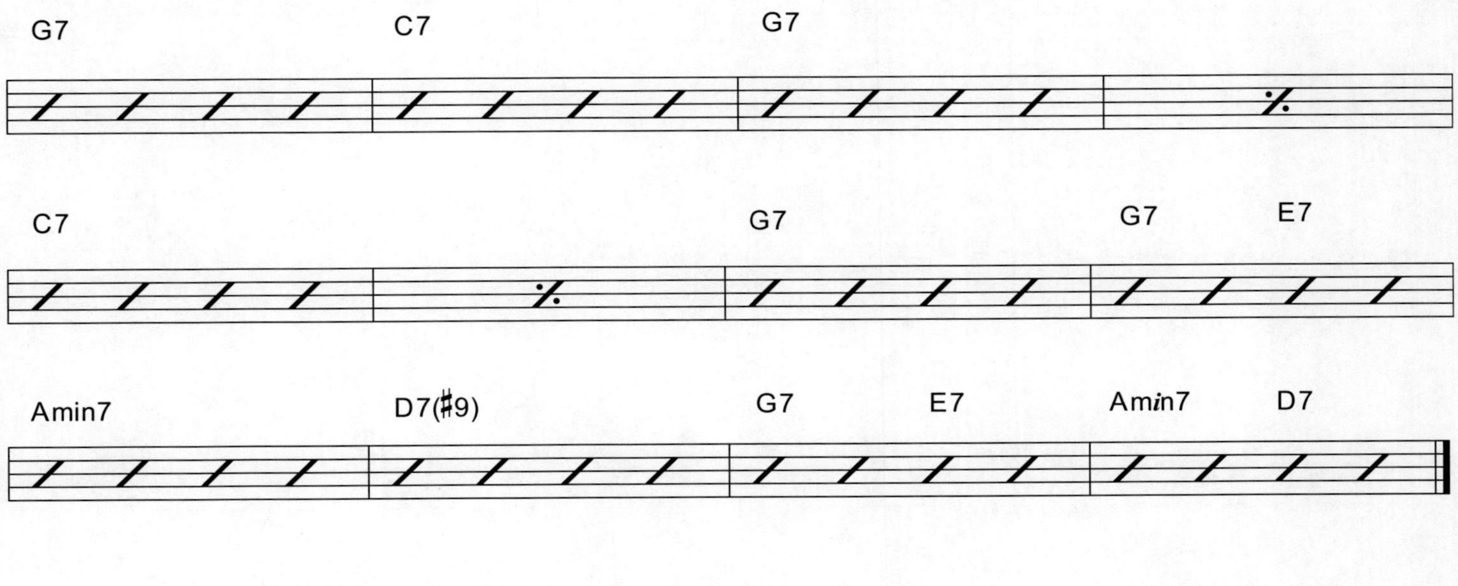

Blue Caboose

16

17 Rhythm Only

Chord Progression

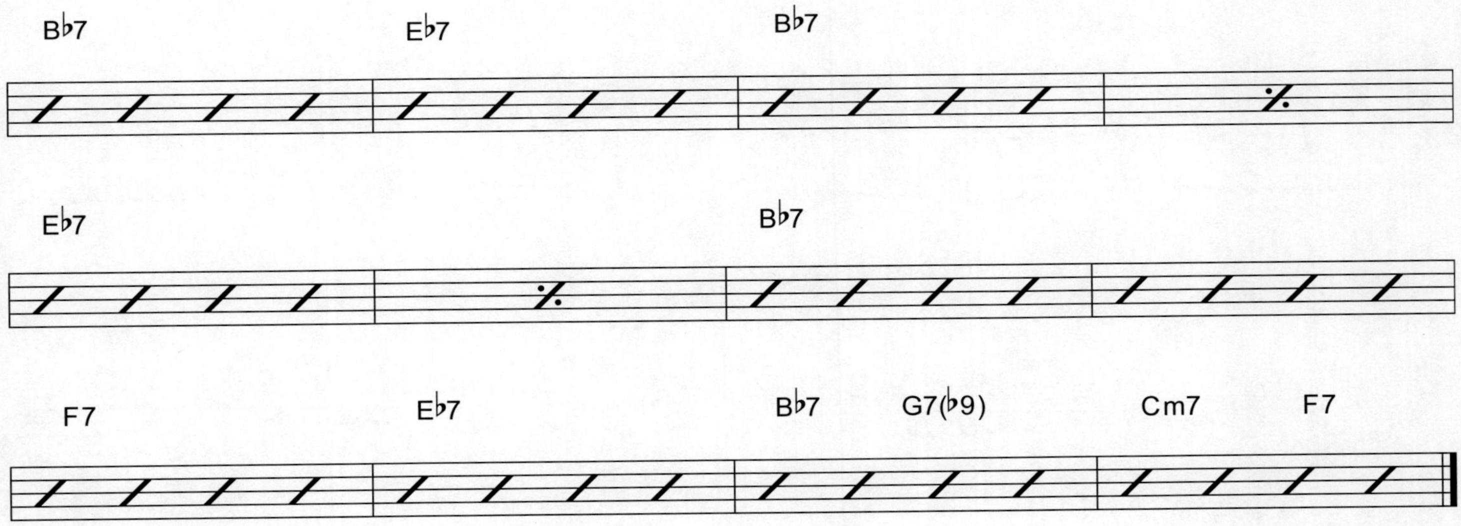

BeBoppin' Alice

Disc 18

Disc 19 Rhythm Only

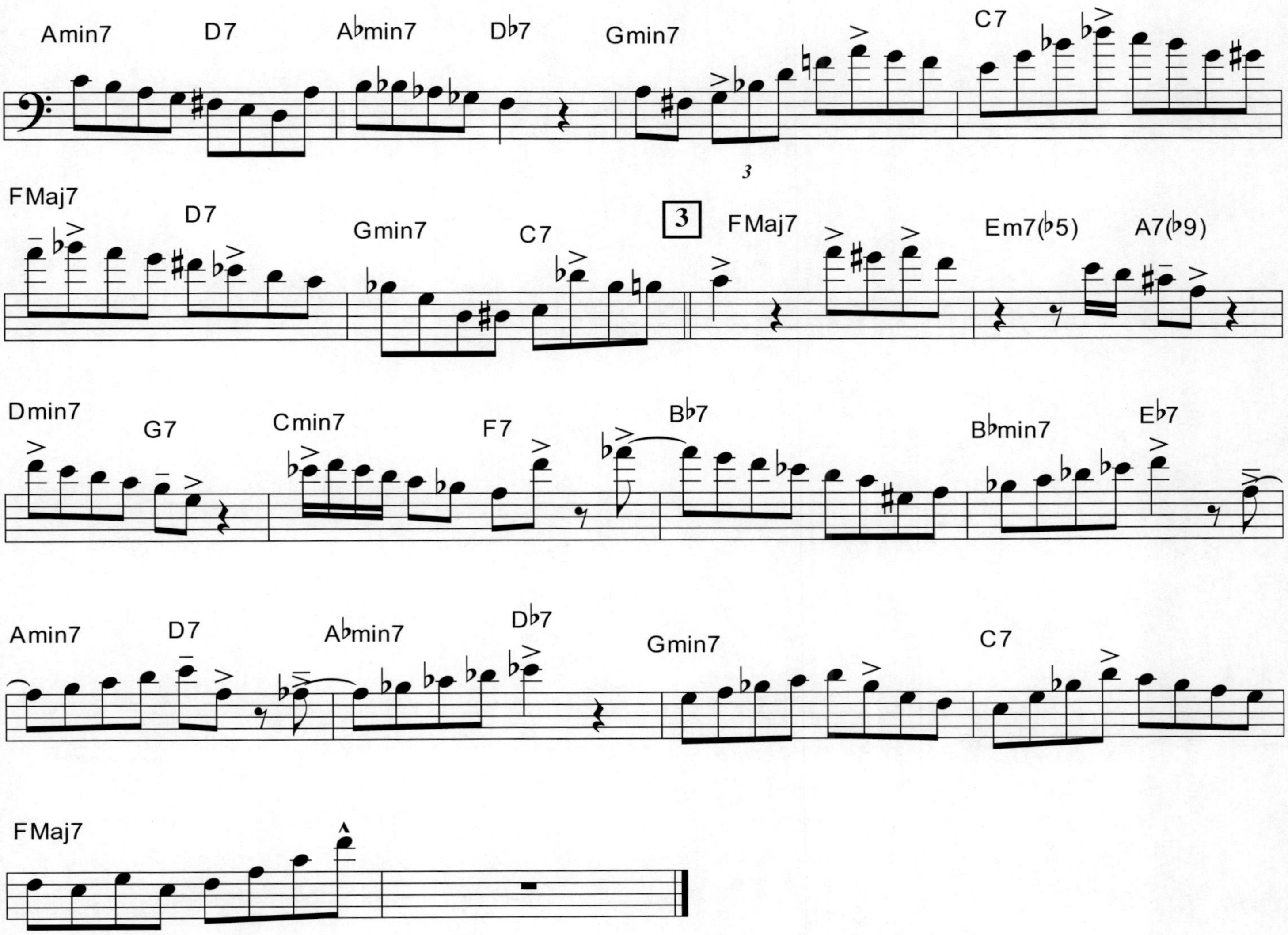

Chord Progression

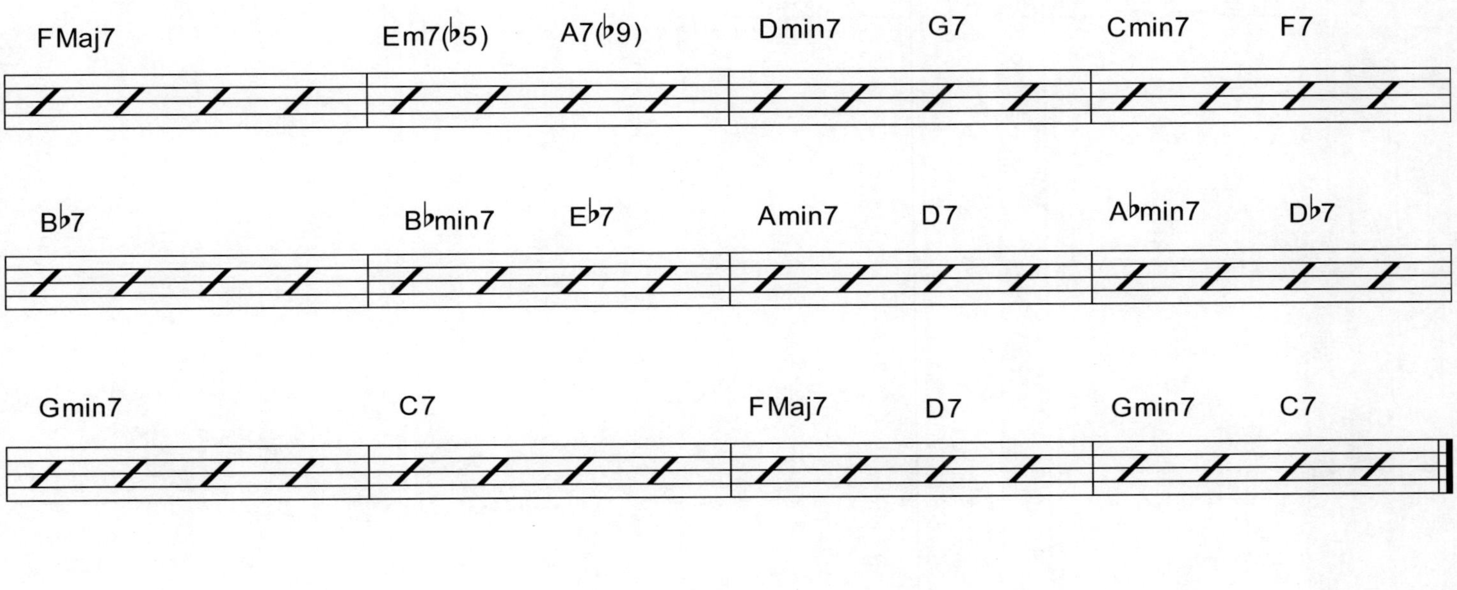

20
21 Rhythm Only

Bouncing Blues

Chord Progression

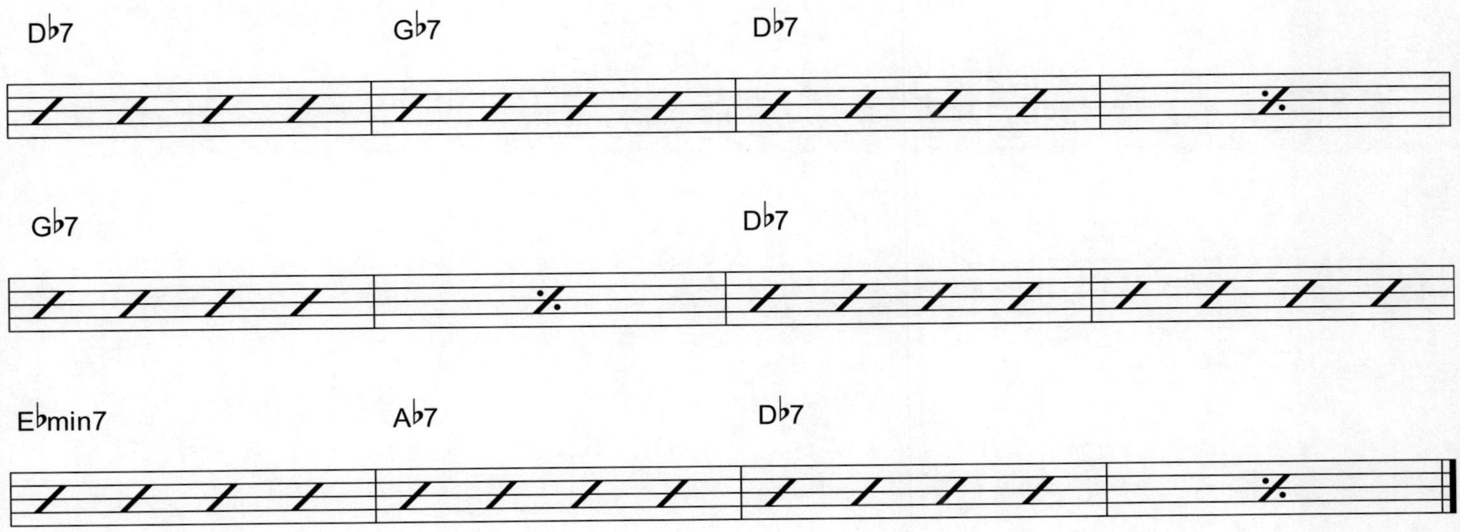

22

23 Rhythm Only

Ursa Minor Blues

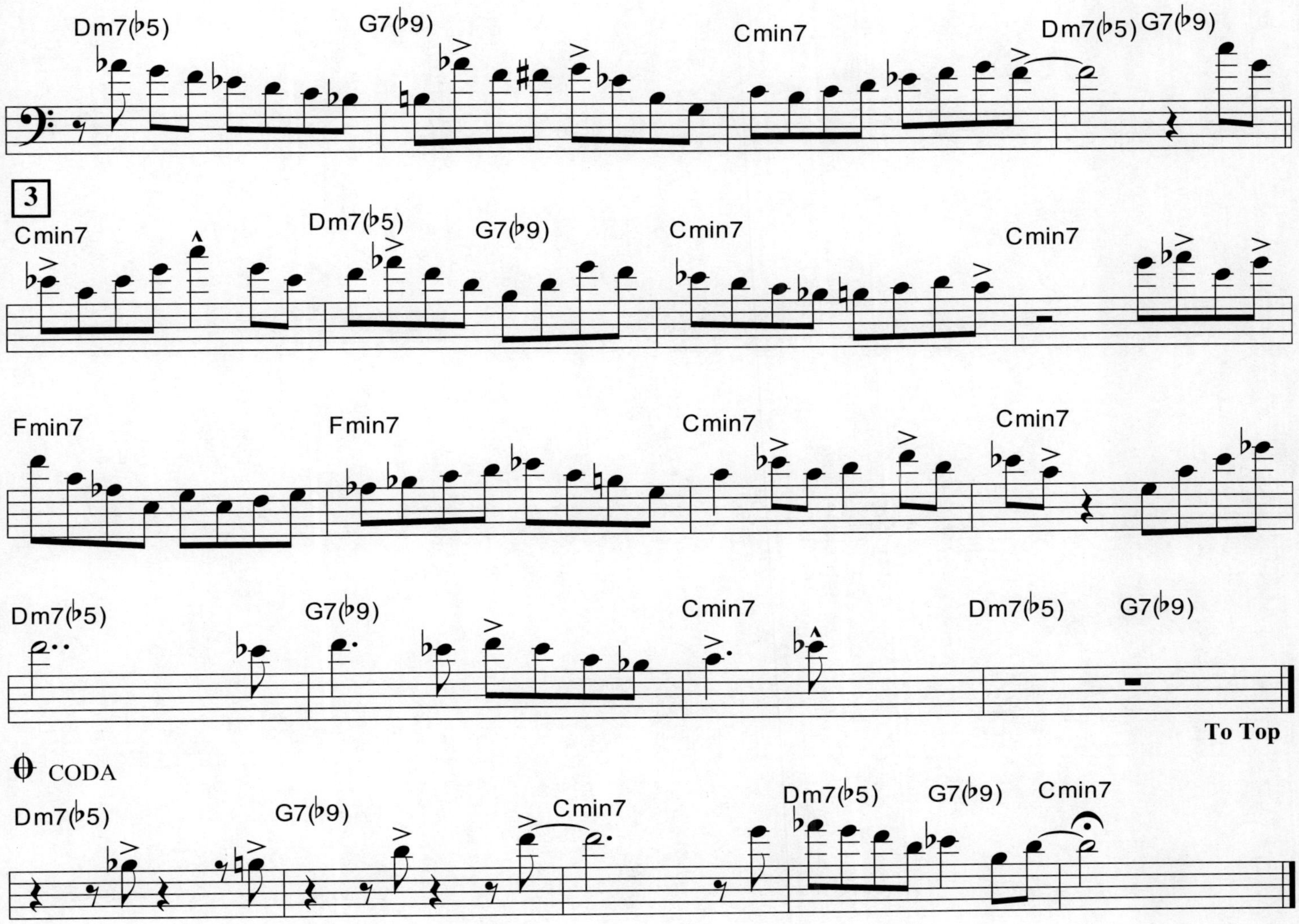

Chord Progression

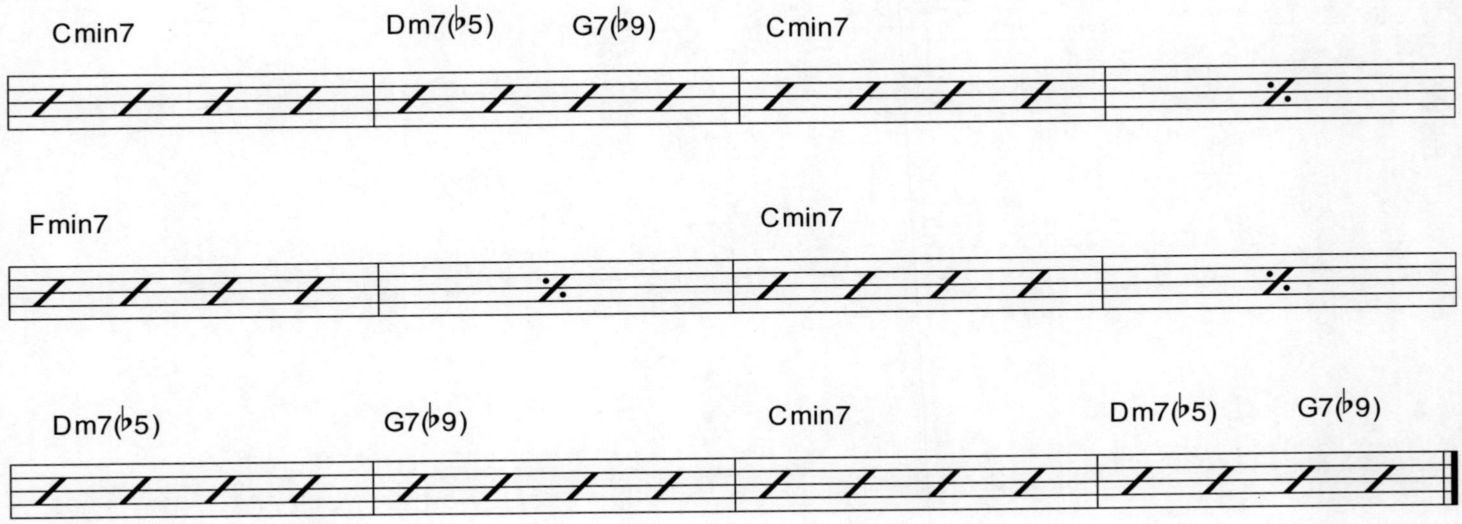

Blues News

24

25 Rhythm Only

Chord Progression

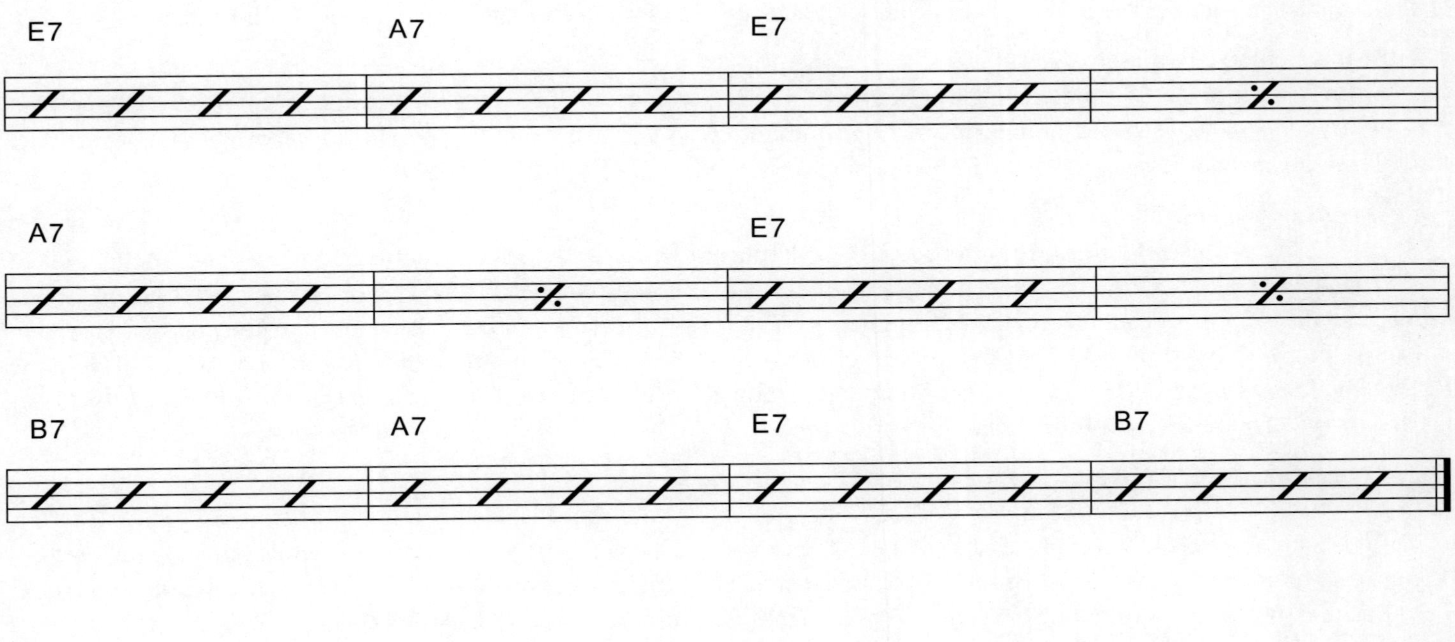

About the Author

Photo by Lorraine Tipaldi

Jack Wilkins, associate professor of jazz studies, did his undergraduate work at the University of Miami and Appalachian State University and received the MM in jazz studies from Indiana University. He previously served on the faculties of Oberlin Conservatory of Music, Appalachian State, and the University of North Carolina. He has performed on saxophone with numerous world-class artists and performing groups including J.J. Johnson, Bobby Shew, Red Rodney, Dianne Shur, the Nelson Riddle Orchestra, and the Cleveland Jazz Orchestra. He has made jazz recordings with Chuck Owen and Jazz Surge, guitarists Bob Ferrazza and Scott Sawyer, pianist Paul Tardis, bassist Matt Kendrick, the Unifour Big Band, David Baker's 21st Century Bebop Band, as well as commercial recordings with various artists including John Mellencamp and Tiny Tim.

A Selmer Instrument Company clinician, Mr. Wilkins is in frequent demand at colleges and high schools across the country for performances and master classes. Jack Wilkins is a member of the International Association for Jazz Education (IAJE) Resource Team, providing expert advice and counsel to the 10,000 plus members of that association. During the summer he serves on the faculty of the Jamey Aebersold Workshops. At USF he is the Director of Jazz Studies, coordinates the jazz chamber ensembles program, teaches jazz improvisation and jazz history, and performs regularly with the USF Faculty Jazz Ensemble. Mr. Wilkins' CD, *Artwork*, released on the Koch Jazz label, received very positive reviews and radio play. Jack's new CD, *Ridgelines* is now out on the ClaveBop label. Both CDs were selected to be featured on *JazzSouth*, a Southern Arts Federation radio program which features prominent southern jazz artists.

The Performers on the CD

Danny Gottlieb, drums

Danny Gottlieb is a familiar name to jazz fans, having served as the original drummer in the Pat Metheny Group. Danny has recorded and performed with many of the greatest jazz artists, and continues to tour and record with a variety of musicians. Between tours and recordings Danny Gottlieb is Artist Faculty at the University of South Florida, and teaches at Rollins College.

Per Danielsson, piano

Per Danielsson is well known in the US and Europe for his jazz piano playing and as a composer/arranger. Originally from Sweden, Per is currently living in Orlando, where he is busy performing, recording, composing and arranging for jazz and commercial projects. Per also has published a series of piano books for Mel Bay including *First Lessons Piano*. Per Danielsson teaches jazz piano and performs with the Faculty Jazz Ensemble at the University of South Florida.

Mark Neuenschwander, bass

Mark Neuenschwander studied music at Memphis State University and has worked in a variety of music settings across the country. Mark has recorded and performed with numerous jazz artists including the latest Jack Wilkins CD release, *Ridgelines*. He teaches bass and plays with University of South Florida Faculty Jazz Ensemble.

Dave Lowry, electric bass

Dave Lowry was self taught from the age of 13. He played with Etta James at Montreux, Switzerland in 1977. Dave received his Professional Diploma in performance from Berklee College of Music in 1981. He played in various touring groups throughout the US and abroad including Aruba and Saudi Arabia from 1981 - 1985. Dave also played in pop jazz fusion groups in Tampa, Florida from 1985 - 1987 and in Las Vegas from 1987 - 1991 with various groups and shows including Clint Holmes. He won the Jazziz Magazine Unsigned Artist Competition judged by John Patitucci for an original bass feature tune *Bass Face*. Dave Lowry currently lives in Florida and plays full-time at Walt Disney World-Epcot, with Morockin.

Tom Brantley, trombone

Tom Brantley is Professor of trombone at the University of South Florida and a member of the touring group, Rhythm and Brass. Tom played lead trombone with the One O'Clock Band at the University of North Texas while pursuing his Masters degree. As a member of Rhythm and Brass Tom composes and performs in a variety of styles and genres from classical to rock. Tom Brantley performs with the USF Faculty Jazz Ensemble and can be heard on Jack Wilkins CD, *Ridgelines*.